FANTASTIC FACTS ABOUT

INCREDIBLE ROBOTS

WARREN SINGER

Cavendish Square

Published in 2026 by Cavendish Square Publishing, LLC
2544 Clinton Street, Buffalo, NY 14224

Website: cavendishsq.com

Author: Warren Singer
Editor: Caroline Thomas
Designer: Redback Publishing

Original illustrations © Redback Publishing 2025
Originated by Redback Publishing

Abbreviations: l—left, r—right, b—bottom, t—top, c—center, m—middle
We would like to thank the following for permission to reproduce photographs: (Images © shutterstock), p4tl MikeDotta/Shutterstock.com, p5tr Anton Gvozdikov/Shutterstock.com, p5bl EBatlleP, CC BY-SA 4.0 <https://creativecommons.org/licenses/by-sa/4.0>, via Wikimedia Commons, p6tr Jihun Sim/Shutterstock.com, p7br nikonka1/Shutterstock.com, p8tl Willrow Hood/Shutterstock.com, p22 MikeDotta/Shutterstock.com, p24mr Ned Snowman/Shutterstock.com, p29br ek robotics GmbH, CC BY-SA 4.0 <https://creativecommons.org/licenses/by-sa/4.0>, via Wikimedia Commons

Cataloging-in-Publication Data

Names: Singer, Warren.
Title: Incredible Robots / Warren Singer.
Description: Buffalo, New York : Cavendish Square Publishing, 2026. |
Series: Fantastic facts about | Includes index and glossary
Identifiers: ISBN 9781502675422 (pbk) | ISBN 9781502675439 (library bound) |
ISBN 9781502675446 (ebook)
Subjects: LCSH: Robots —Juvenile Literature | Robotics --Juvenile Literature
Classification: LCC TJ211.2 S55 2026 | DDC 629.892 --dc25

CPSIA compliance information: Batch #CSCSQ26: For further information contact Cavendish Square Publishing LLC at 1-877-980-4450.

Printed in the United States of America

CONTENTS

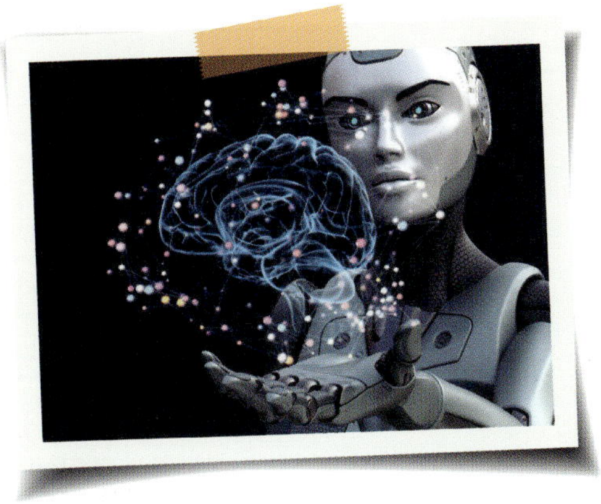

Quick Facts

These quick facts will get you started on your quest to find out all you want to know about robots.

WHAT IS A ROBOT?

A robot is a machine that can perform tasks without having to be directed what to do at every step. They can do the work that humans either cannot do, or do not want to do.

ARTIFICIAL INTELLIGENCE

Modern robots are controlled by computer programs and rely on AI (artificial intelligence) to make their own decisions about what actions to take.

WHEN WERE ROBOTS INVENTED?

People have been making mechanical devices to do work for hundreds of years. A wind-up clock is a sort of robot because it can go on doing its job as long as it has power from the tightly-wound spring inside it.

DO ALL ROBOTS LOOK LIKE A HUMAN?

A robot does not need to look like a person to do its work, but we still instantly imagine a humanoid machine when we think of robots. Scientists design some robots to look humanoid (like a human), or to speak as though they were really alive. This helps us to interact with robots more easily.

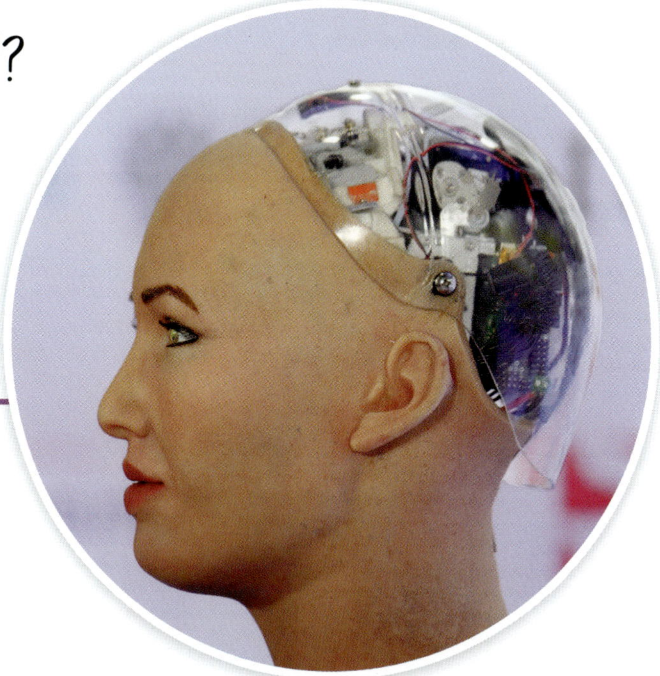

WHO DESIGNS ROBOTS?

Making a robot involves the input of many trained people. They include computer coders, mechanical engineers, and psychologists. Psychologists are people who study how humans behave. This allows them to work out the best way for a humanoid robot to appear to be safe and friendly.

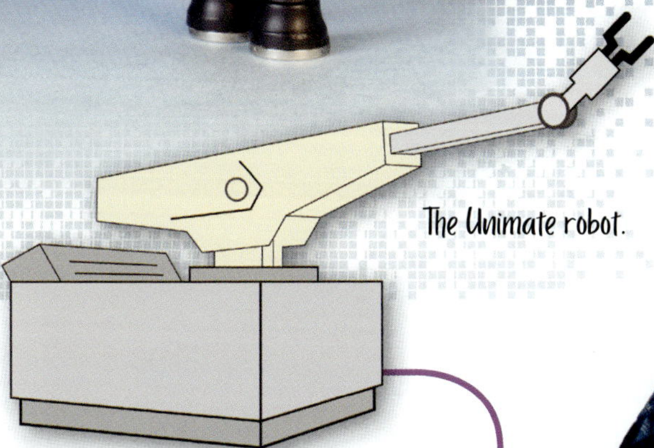

The Unimate robot.

FIRST FACTORY ROBOT

Unimate was the first industrial robot that was electronically controlled. It was invented in the mid-1900s.

Humanoid Robots

THEY LOOK ALIVE!

While some manufacturers design their robots to be functional, such as those that do factory work, others are attempting to make their robots look just like people. These sorts of robots do not look threatening, so they can take on the role of friends or helpers in homes, businesses, and healthcare, without scaring people.

A robot receptionist at the reception desk of a Henna Na Hotel in Tokyo.

CHATBOTS

Chatbots are robots that speak to us or write responses to answer questions, usually about a product or service that we have found online. Chatbots are humanoid robots, because they are designed to sound and react like a real person, even though they have no actual robot body that we can see.

ARTIFICIAL INTELLIGENCE

Modern robots rely on AI, artificial intelligence, to perform their tasks in ways that look lifelike. The coding used for robots is no longer just a sequence of steps allowing a humanoid machine to do one task, such as picking up a cup.

Using AI, software engineers now design robots that make their own decisions about what to do next, based on events happening around them, just like humans do.

ARMS AND LEGS

Humanoid robots have a face, arms, and legs even though these features of a real person may not be the best way to perform a robotic job. For example, helping a patient in a hospital to stand up might be better done with a robot that does not look human and that has been designed to lift in a different and safer way. Despite this, the effect on a sick person of being lifted by a machine that looks dangerous could be very negative.

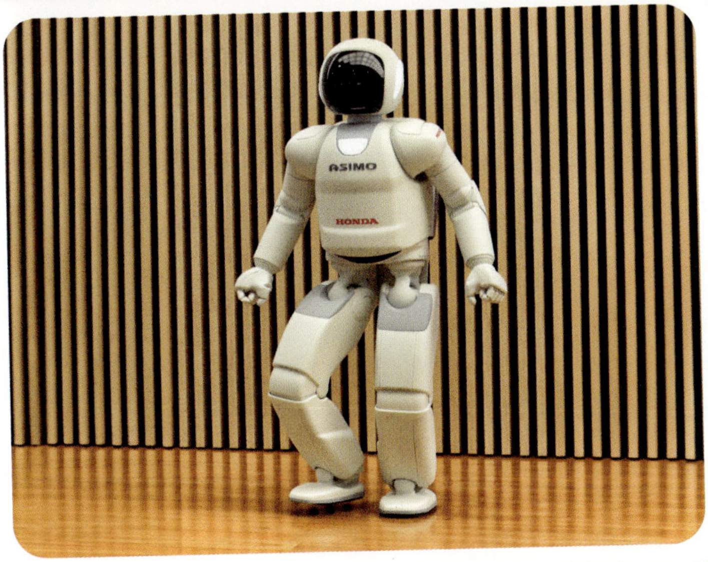

Will Humans Become Robots?

IS IT HUMAN?

Movies and stories sometimes include robot characters that have feelings and behave like humans. A robot that depends on artificial intelligence for all its actions, and is not using any living parts to exist, is not human. At least, that's what we think now. What people of the distant future will answer to such a question could be different, as robots advance in sophistication.

ROBOTIC REPLACEMENT PARTS

Humans can already have parts of their bodies assisted by mechanical implants and devices. We can imagine a time in the future when the normal lifespan of a person will be increased due to the use of robotic replacement organs and other body parts.

WHO IS IN CONTROL?

If a future human has robotic implants that make their body do things they do not want, who would be guilty if they committed a crime? The ethics of robot behavior are serious considerations for experts in robotics. Robot capabilities are advancing so quickly, it is difficult to know what will be possible in the near or distant future.

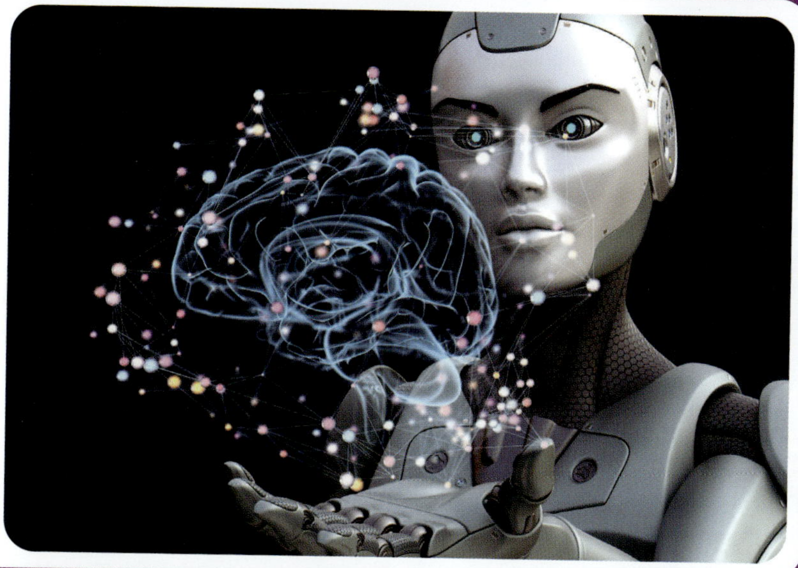

HUMAN OR ROBOT?

At what point does a human become a robot and no longer human? If a brain could be replaced with a computer, would this make the whole person a robot or a human?

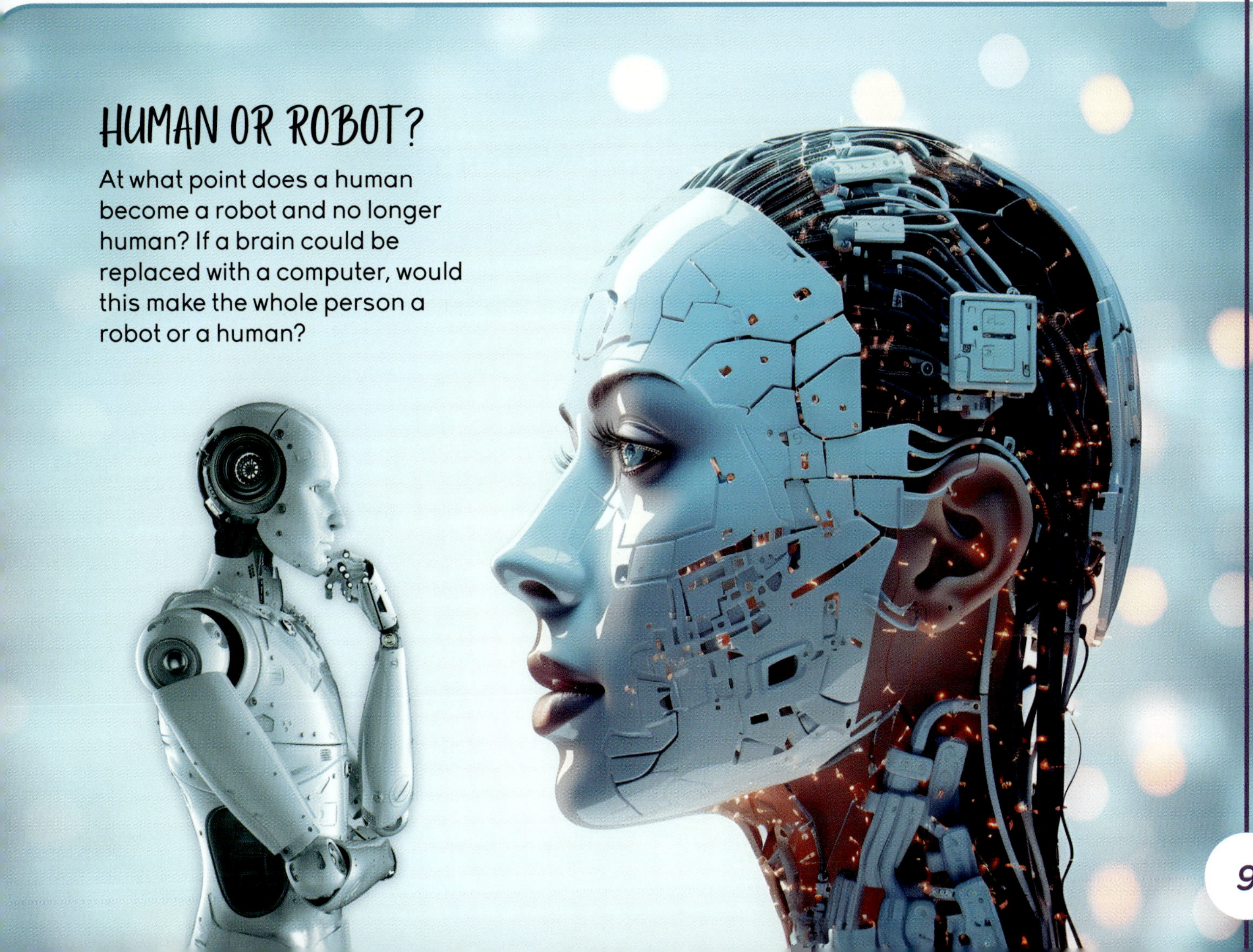

Are Robots Safe?

IT'S ALL ABOUT THE CODING

Robots do tasks using coding written by people. If the coding contains errors that cause the robot to behave in dangerous ways, all sorts of unwanted outcomes can occur.

When the coding involves giving a robot the ability to create its own code, then it might make decisions that were not planned by its human coders.

CAGED ROBOTS

In factories where robots perform dangerous assembly jobs, they are sometimes contained in cages, just in case something goes wrong. Robots move so quickly compared with a human, that just doing their ordinary job can result in them causing injury to a slower human nearby.

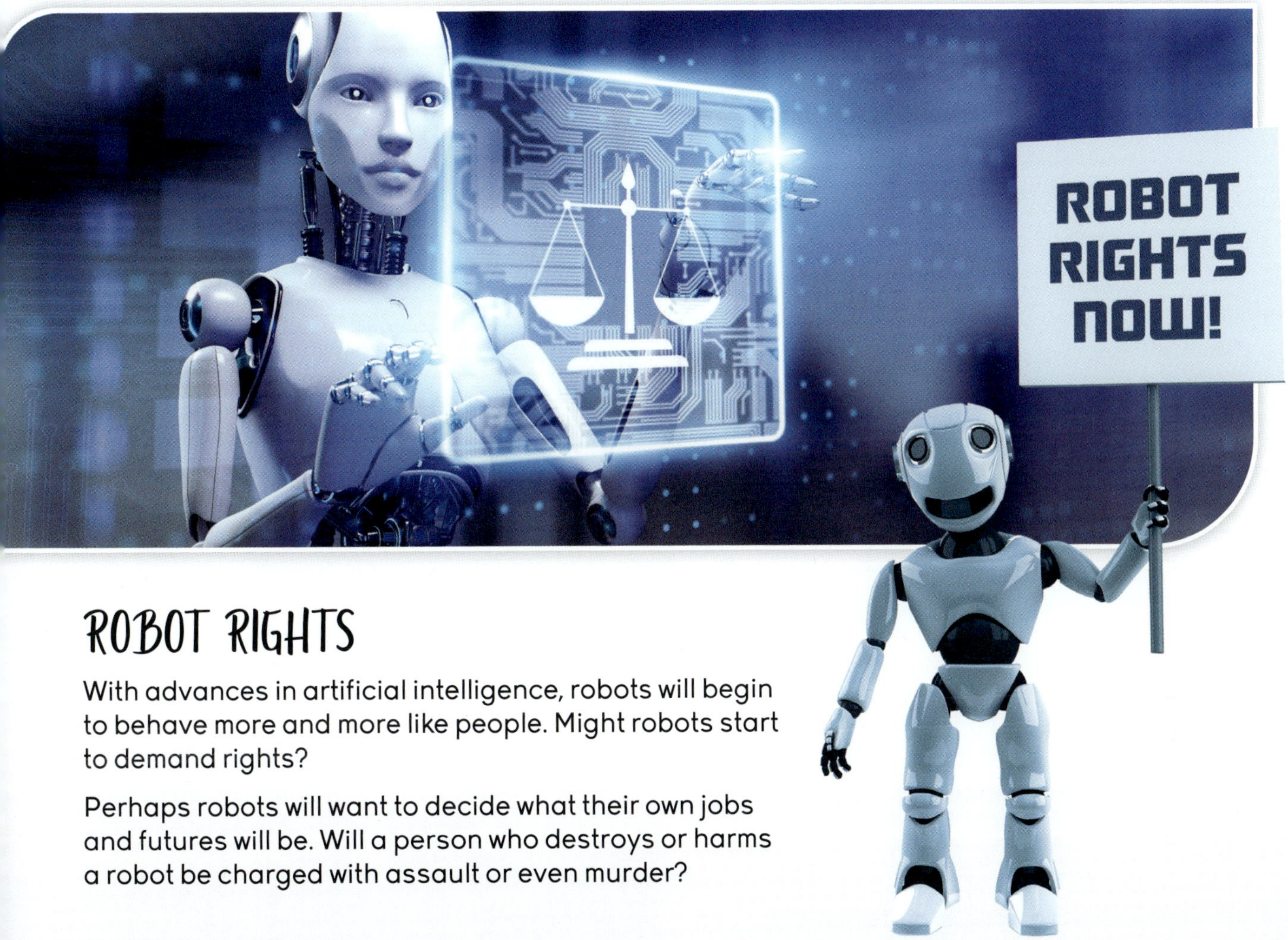

ROBOT RIGHTS

With advances in artificial intelligence, robots will begin to behave more and more like people. Might robots start to demand rights?

Perhaps robots will want to decide what their own jobs and futures will be. Will a person who destroys or harms a robot be charged with assault or even murder?

ROBOT RULES OF BEHAVIOR

The so-called laws of robotics were written by a science fiction writer, Isaac Asimov, in 1942. The basis of his rules was that humans must never be harmed by a robot. There are no real laws about robot behavior, and there are many military robots built whose aim is to destroy an enemy, whether it is a human or another robot.

Science fiction writer Isaac Asimov

Robots and Health

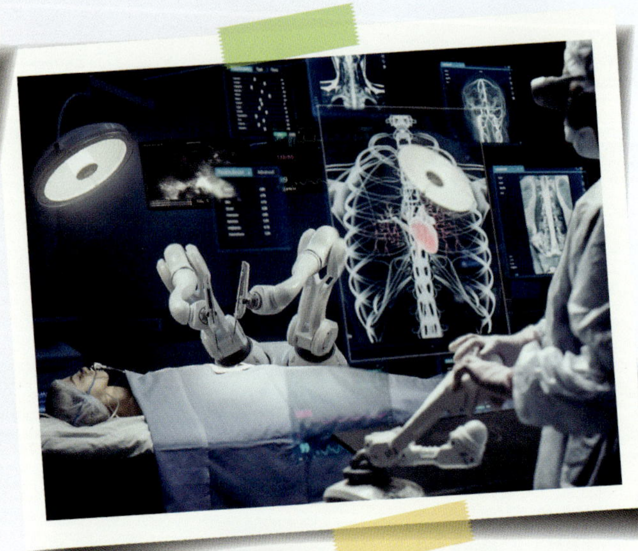

HEALTHCARE AND MEDICINE

In the future, robots may be able to do much of the healthcare work that is now done by health technicians, nurses, and even doctors. These jobs could include giving injections, taking blood samples, performing operations and dentistry, and analyzing symptoms to make a diagnosis of what illness a patient has.

TRANSLATORS

In multicultural societies, there are many people who speak different languages. A humanoid robot translator can make a patient feel more at ease, and help the medical staff to understand what the patient is telling them. Since it is impossible to have a human who speaks every world language, a robot can be an efficient alternative.

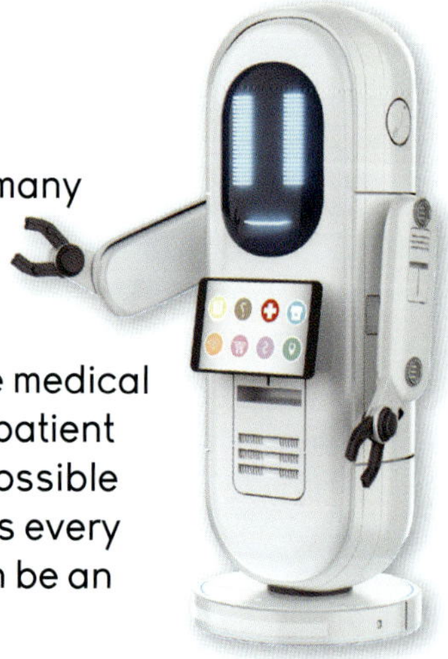

ELDER CARE

The world's population is aging in many countries. Robots may be able to take over the care of frail, elderly people, since there will not be enough younger people to do all the elder care work that will be needed in the future.

LONELINESS

Even though the world's population is increasing every day, loneliness is also increasing amongst people of all ages. Humanoid robots may be able to assist by providing companionship, someone to talk to or dance with, and even a partner in a chess or board game.

Small Robots

NANOBOTS IN MEDICINE

Some robots might be so tiny that we could only see them under a microscope. They could be used in the future to cure diseases by repairing our DNA, or attacking bacteria and viruses. These nanobots could possibly be made of biological material rather than metals, but who knows what the future will bring?

NANOBOTS IN INDUSTRY

Nanobots might also be used in manufacturing to work with dangerous substances or to work with precise accuracy.

DRONES

Small, flying drones first became popular as toys and as ways to view a landscape from the air. Drones have now evolved to be one of the main weapons used by armies fighting a battle.

These sorts of drones are called UCAVs (unmanned combat aerial vehicles), and they can carry missiles and bombs very close to their targets. Other advantages of drones as weapons is that they do not need a human pilot, and they are smaller and less expensive than aircraft.

Home Robots

Here are some examples of real robots that can help at home:

NOT HUMANOID

When the idea of robot helpers in the home was first discussed in the mid-1900s, people imagined that the robot would look like a person and would do all the housework in the same way that a person does.

Home assistants such as Siri, Alexa, and Google Assistant

Robot that folds laundry

Robot window cleaner

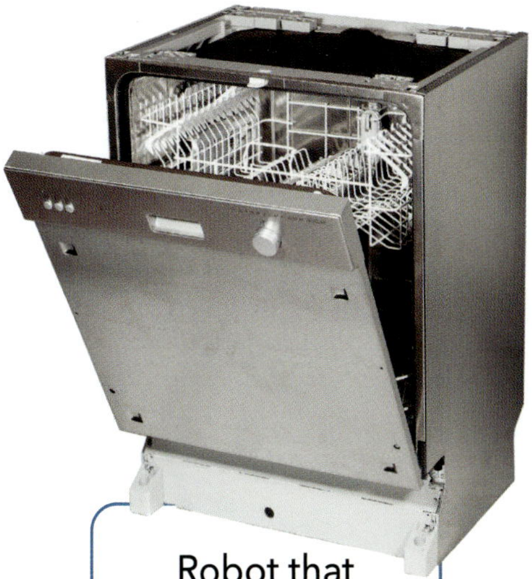

Robot that washes dishes

HOME HELP

Robots are now common in households in many countries, but they do not look like a metal maid who does the housework. There are different robots for each task, and they are not humanoid.

Robot vacuum cleaners

Robot lawn mowers

Robot Cars

EMERGENCY!

Some cars have AI features such as automatic emergency braking and collision avoidance. The car's computer does thousands of calculations to make its own decisions about what it should do to stop an accident from happening, while also protecting the driver of the car.

SELF-DRIVING

Self-driving cars need to be aware of everything that is going on around them. However, any glitch in the car's software may be magnified in its effect if the car is traveling at high speed. A self-driving car's movement could be supervised by a human driver, or the car might travel using only its own artificial intelligence.

Pedestrian detection is a vital feature of self-driving cars

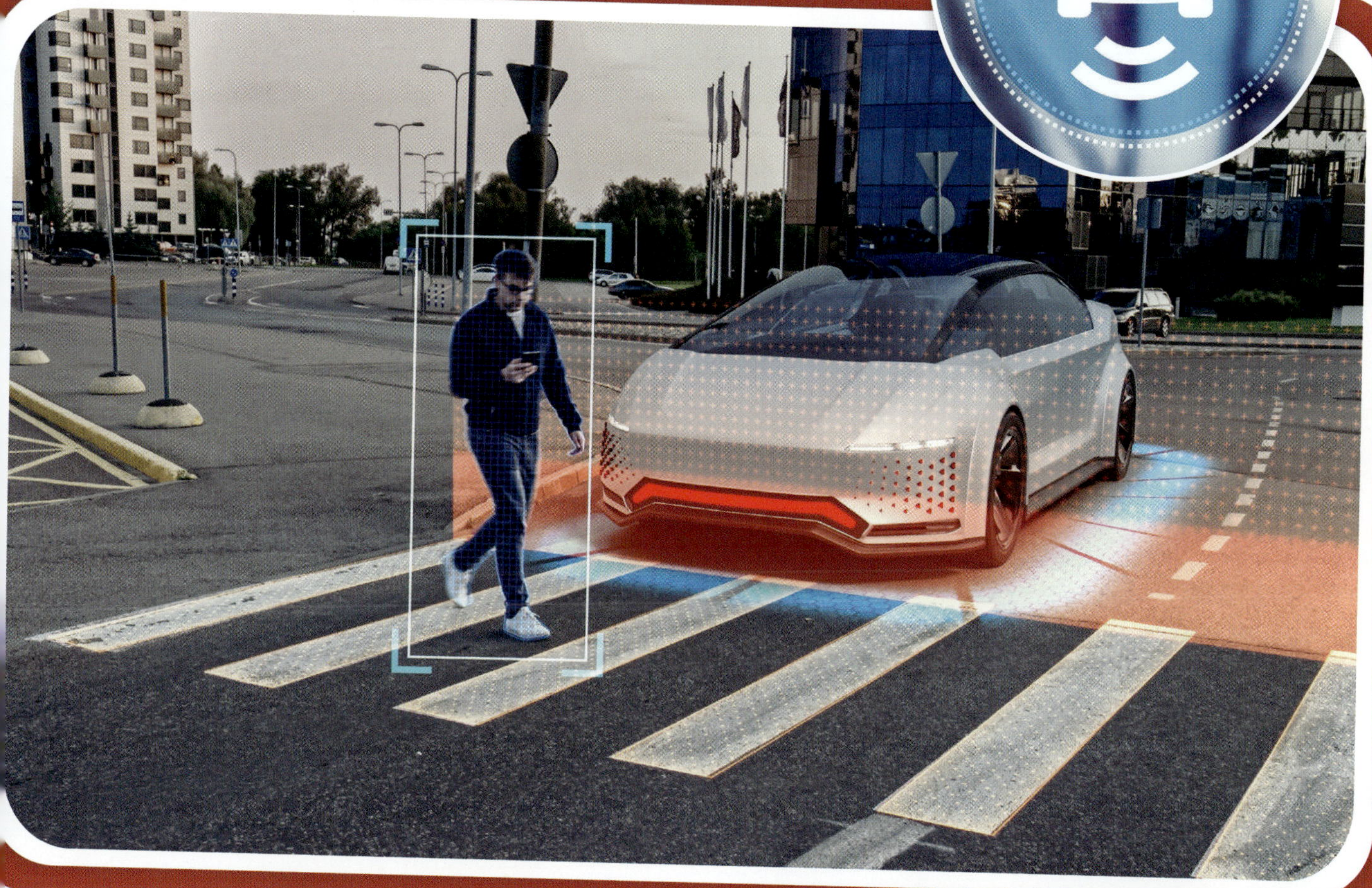

AI IN CARS

Modern cars include these artificial intelligence (AI) features:

- Collision avoidance
- Pedestrian detection
- Lane departure warning
- Cruise control
- Engine health monitoring

To do all these actions, AI needs to collect sensory data, just as humans do. The car's sensors include movement and temperature detectors, radar, distance calculators, and cameras.

Robots in Science Fiction

SCARY SCI-FI

Writers and movie-makers have depicted robots in a range of scenarios. Gigantic metallic monsters, huge AI insects, or creatures with metal armor and a living brain are just some terrifying examples.

Until recently, many people believed that these imagined robots might be the only reality. Thankfully, advances in robotics science have now produced robots that do not look frightening, are appropriately sized, and are genuinely helpful to humans. The general public also knows more about how robots really work, and children learn to code robotic movements at school.

FROM FICTION TO REALITY

The advanced sensory abilities and strength of fictional robots made them scary and fascinating at the same time. Although the skills of these robots once seemed too advanced to ever really exist, AI and robotic engineering are now developing so rapidly that the gap between reality and fiction is narrowing.

Animal Robots

QUADRUPEDS

Having four legs gives a walking robot a lot of stability. These sorts of robots are designed to carry loads and travel over a rough surface. They can be used in a battle situation to deliver supplies to soldiers.

Equipped with GPS, four-legged robots might also be used in the future to make package deliveries, or to act as guard dogs.

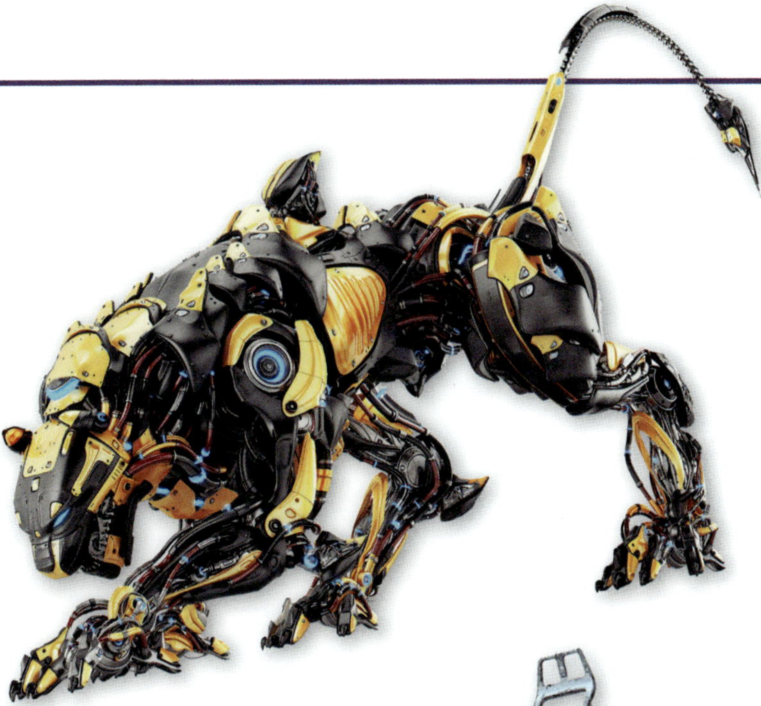

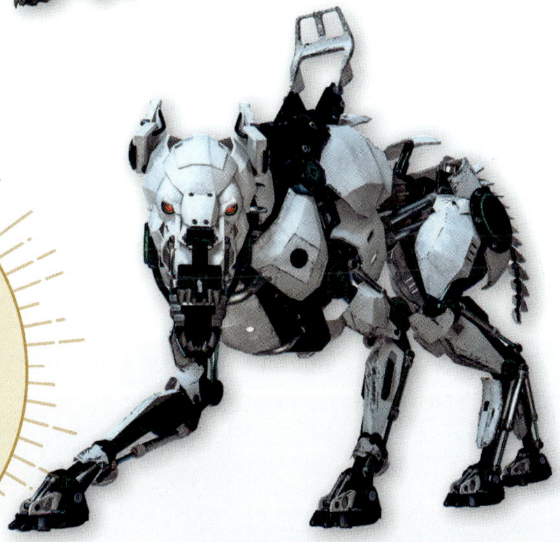

COMING SOON?

Animal robots of the future could be beautiful, deadly, and awesome, just like real animals!

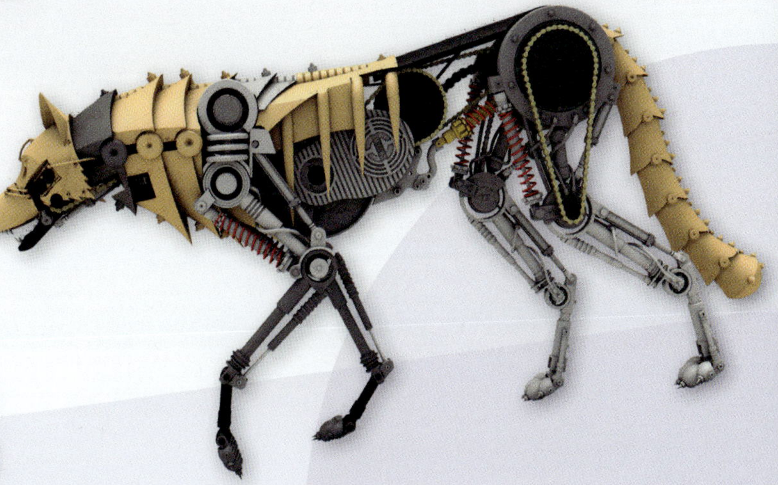

Robots and Kids

ROBOT CREATURES

Robotic animal toys can respond to a child's words and actions. Designers try to make these toys behave just like a pet dog or cat, by moving their head, paws, or eyes in the same way that a pet animal does.

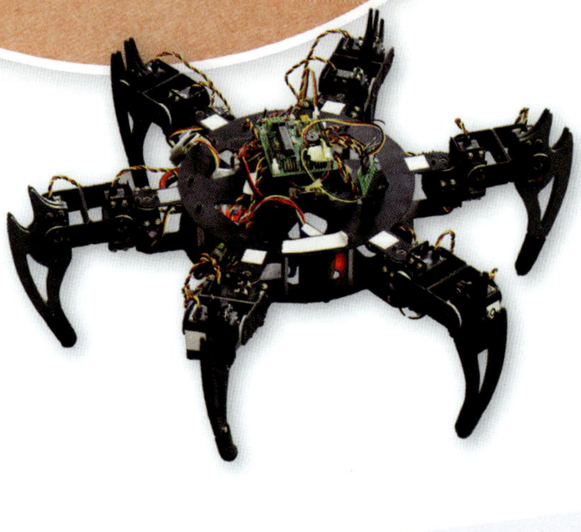

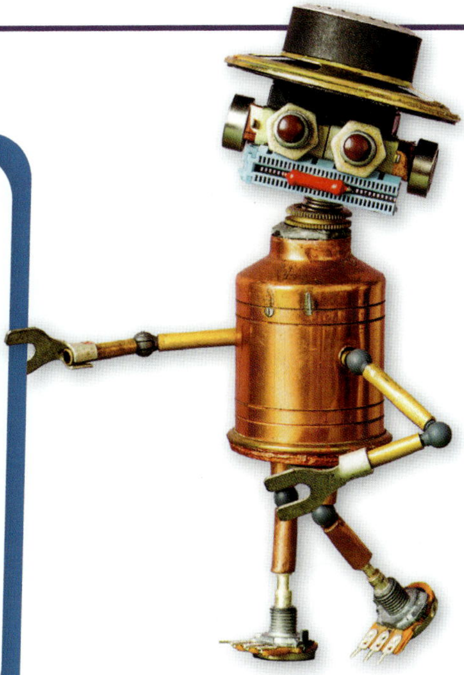

COMICAL ROBOTS

Some robots are designed to look funny or sad. They are more like pets or friends than metal monsters.

Creators of cartoon robots like to give their mechanical characters feelings that a real robot could not produce.

Robot Insects and Spiders

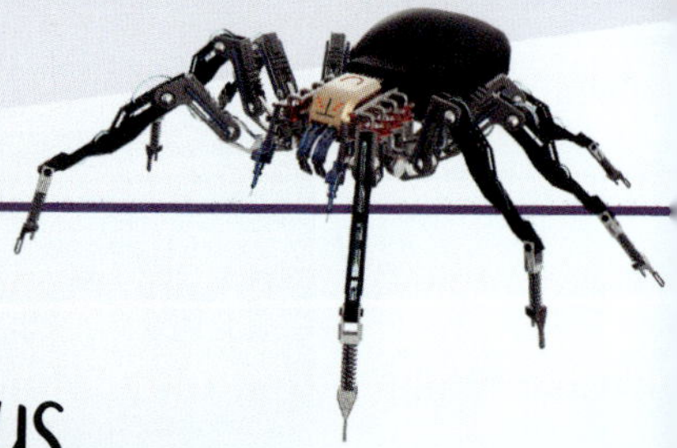

TINY BUT DANGEROUS

Battle robots are usually shown in movies and illustrations as being large and humanoid, but robots can also be tiny. A swarm of flying, robotic insects, or scuttling spiders, could create as much damage in a battle as a large, metal soldier.

A swarm of tiny, fierce robots is a horrifying possibility. They would be difficult to destroy, and their effects could be devastating.

SOLVING PROBLEMS

Software engineers have looked at the swarming behavior of real insects to understand how to create a robotic swarm. Each individual in a swarm of tiny robots could communicate with those around it, and all of them would then learn from each other.

Factory Robots

DANGEROUS JOBS

Many of the robots in the world are at work in dangerous factory surroundings. They move heavy items, weld metal, and deal with poisonous chemicals. They can do this all day and night without stopping, making them more productive than a human at these types of jobs. Robots can work much faster than a human, and they don't need lunch breaks.

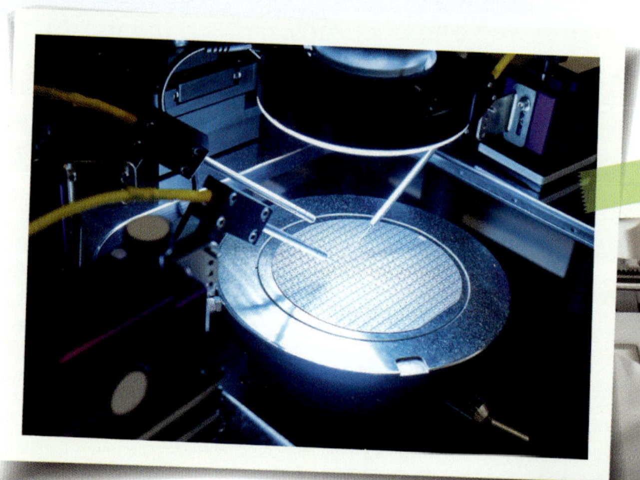

Silicon chip construction

An automated blood testing analysis machine

PRECISION LABORATORY JOBS

Robots are very good at performing repetitive tasks that need constant attention to fine detail. These jobs include checking blood tests from humans, or making silicon chips.

MAKING MACHINERY

The widespread use of robots in making cars is an example of machines making machines. Robots do these jobs with speed and accuracy, making the finished product more likely to be free from construction errors.

ROBOTS PRODUCING FOOD

Robots are now used in all parts of the food production chain, from growing crops, milking cows, and collecting eggs, to processing, packing, and dispatching the finished product. An advantage in using robots in food production is that they can be disinfected and they do not carry diseases that can be spread to food.

The Future of Robots

In the future, it is likely that robots will appear in more and more aspects of our lives. This will certainly result in the loss of work for some people, but new work opportunities will open up as well.

Skilled software engineers, and people with a clear vision of what humanity needs to go forward, will help to ensure robots develop to serve the needs of humanity, rather than standing in our way.

No one knows for certain how humans and robots will interact in the future, but the possibilities for improved health and more efficient use of resources are exciting.

Glossary

AI artificial intelligence produced by computer coding

chatbot computer-generated voice or text that answers queries

diagnosis decision about the nature of an illness based on symptoms

DNA genetic material that determines how life develops

ethically with regard to what is right and wrong

ethics study of what is right and wrong and why

frail having not much energy and poor health

GPS global positioning system used for locating people or things

humanoid like a human

implant artificial device or living tissue placed within a body

interact communicate and share ideas and information

missile explosive weapon sent to a target

nanobots microscopic-sized robots

psychologist person who studies how humans behave

quadruped animal or robot having four legs

sophistication high level of understanding and competence

UCAV unmanned combat aerial vehicle

weld join metals by heating and melting them

Index

TITLES IN THIS SERIES

AI: ARTIFICIAL INTELLIGENCE

INCREDIBLE ROBOTS

MAGNIFICENT OCEANS

SPECTACULAR SPACE

Cavendish Square

ISBN: 9781502675422

9 781502 675422